ALTERNATOR BOOKS™

SURVIVING
A CANYON

ARON
RALSTON

KATIE MARSICO

Lerner Publications ◆ Minneapolis

To Maria, CJ, Thomas, Megan, Abby, and Lauren—the six bravest people I know

Lerner Publications Company
A division of Lerner Publishing Group, Inc.
241 First Avenue North
Minneapolis, MN USA 55401

For reading levels and more information, look up this title at www.lernerbooks.com.

Library of Congress Cataloging-in-Publication Data

Names: Marsico, Katie, 1980– author.
Title: Surviving a canyon : Aron Ralston / Katie Marsico.
Description: Minneapolis : Lerner Publications, [2018] | Series: They Survived (Alternator Books) | Includes bibliographical references and index. | Audience: Ages: 8–12. | Audience: Grades: 4 to 6.
Identifiers: LCCN 2018005334 (print) | LCCN 2017041219 (ebook) | ISBN 9781541525603 (eb pdf) | ISBN 9781541523517 (lb : alk. paper)
Subjects: LCSH: Ralston, Aron—Juvenile literature. | Rock climbing accidents—Utah—Canyonlands National Park—Juvenile literature. | Mountaineering accidents—Utah—Canyonlands National Park—Juvenile literature. | Survival—Utah—Canyonlands National Park—Juvenile literature. | Mountaineers—United States—Biography—Juvenile literature.
Classification: LCC GV199.42.U82 (print) | LCC GV199.42.U82 C345 2018 (ebook) | DDC 796.522/30979259—dc23

LC record available at https://lccn.loc.gov/2018005334

Manufactured in the United States of America
1-44424-34683-5/9/2018

CONTENTS

INTRODUCTION
TRAPPED

Aron Ralston stared up from the depths of Bluejohn Canyon in Utah. The twenty-seven-year-old was an experienced hiker. But nothing could have prepared him for this. He was trapped.

A huge boulder smashed Ralston's right hand and wrist against the canyon wall. He was alone. He didn't have a cell phone with him, and he was in a **remote** part of the desert. He had some tools and a little food and water, but his supplies wouldn't last forever. If Ralston wasn't rescued—or if he couldn't free himself—would he survive?

CHAPTER 1

AN UNPLANNED ADVENTURE

Ralston loved not being able to guess every twist and turn in an adventure. It was one of the reasons he had become a professional mountain climber. Ralston had worked as a mechanical engineer at Intel, a well-known technology company. Then, in 2002, he decided he wanted a career involving the wilderness. He moved to Aspen, Colorado, where he found a job at an outdoor-gear store. He often hiked or climbed on his days off.

Ralston and a few of his friends had scheduled a climbing **expedition** for the final week of April 2003. At the last minute, however, they canceled the trip. So Ralston planned his own adventure.

Normally, if Ralston was hiking alone, he left a detailed note for his roommates, telling them of his plans. That way, they would know how to reach him in an emergency. But this time, Ralston didn't have a precise schedule when he left home. He knew only that he would be in Utah.

Ralston climbed Capitol Peak in Colorado on his own in February 2003.

On Saturday morning, April 26, 2003, Ralston parked his truck about 8 miles (13 km) north of Bluejohn Canyon. He wore a baseball cap, T-shirt, shorts, wool socks, and running shoes. He headed out on his mountain bike, carrying a 25-pound (11 kg) pack on his back. He had food, water, a headlamp, and **rappelling** tools. He also had headphones, a CD player, CDs, a digital camera, a mini digital video recorder, and batteries. It was plenty for a daylong exploration.

Bluejohn Canyon has become a popular destination for canyoneering, a sport that involves hiking and rappelling.

SURVIVAL GEAR

It is important to bring plenty of water on outdoor expeditions to avoid **dehydration**. Ralston carried a water bottle and a hydration pack. A hydration pack looks like a backpack with a rubber or plastic container for water. Hikers drink through a hose connected to the container. Hydration packs store more liquid than a regular water bottle and are easy to carry. Many are also insulated to prevent water from freezing or becoming too warm.

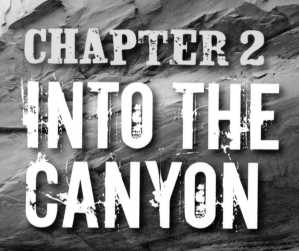

CHAPTER 2
INTO THE
CANYON

After riding dusty trails all morning, Ralston locked his bike to a tree and began his climb. Occasionally, he paused to take photographs of the sandstone walls around him. As Ralston snapped one last picture, he noticed the time stamp on his camera—2:41 p.m. That moment would remain burned into his mind for years to come.

Ralston started his descent through the narrow space in the canyon. He moved carefully among the rocks, climbing over boulders and ledges. He tested each one to make sure it would hold his weight. But as he hung from a boulder he had just climbed over, about to drop to the canyon floor, he felt the boulder begin to move. He jumped away and threw his hands up, and then everything seemed to move in slow motion. There was a moment of darkness as the 800-pound (363 kg) rock fell toward him. It seemed to block all the light in the canyon. Then came a flood of piercing pain as the rock crushed his arm and hand against the canyon wall.

Ralston was trapped in this narrow space in the canyon.

Ralston's arm was pinned between this boulder and the canyon wall.

Ralston frantically tried pulling his arm loose. He shoved at the boulder with his free hand, but the rock didn't budge. Ralston was tired, sweaty, and thirsty. As he took a drink, it suddenly occurred to him that he couldn't waste his water supply. If he did, his odds of survival would be slim.

In less than an hour, Ralston lost all the feeling in his right hand. He took off his pack and used his left arm to sort through his supplies. He had two small burritos, a few muffin crumbs, and 22 ounces (0.7 L) of water. In the past, Ralston had been on outdoor expeditions where he'd survived six days without food. But he wouldn't last half as long without water. Dehydration would set in quickly in the dry desert heat. During the day, the rocks around Ralston would bake in the sun. Once night fell, temperatures would dip. In his T-shirt and shorts, Ralston wasn't dressed for cool weather. The cold and discomfort would make sleep almost impossible. Once his water was gone, Ralston knew he might die in one to three days.

Temperatures can drop more than 30°F (17°C) when the sun goes down in the Canyonlands.

CHAPTER 3
A WAY OUT

Ralston knew that if another hiker didn't come by, he had three possible ways out of the canyon. Ralston often used the blade on his **multi-tool** to carve rock so it was easier to grip and climb. He thought he might be able to chip away at the boulder and free himself. Or he might create a pulley system to move the boulder. His third option was to **amputate** his hand.

With his left hand, Ralston held the multi-tool and hammered at the rock. But the boulder was much harder than the rocks Ralston normally cut into. All he managed to do was wear down his blade. Within about a day, he knew he wouldn't be able to free himself this way. When he tried to build a

Ralston used a tool similar to this one to try to cut into the rock.

pulley with rope and other rappelling equipment, he quickly realized the boulder was too heavy to move.

Ralston had been carefully **rationing** supplies since Saturday. But on Tuesday, he ran out of food and water. He began to sense things that weren't real. By Wednesday, Ralston imagined that his friends were visiting him. It even sounded as if his mother was calling his name.

Franco works on a scene for *127 Hours*, showing Ralston's actions after becoming trapped in the canyon.

SURVIVAL GEAR

Most people wouldn't view a video recorder as survival gear. But it was the closest thing Ralston had to human contact. He didn't know if or when he'd next see his family and friends, so he started taping messages to his loved ones. His recordings also helped him keep track of time, organize his thoughts, and develop a survival plan.

Ralston knew he had to amputate if he hoped to live. To avoid bleeding to death, he made a **tourniquet** from a metal climbing clip and the insulation from the tube on his hydration pack. He prepared to cut into his arm. But he discovered the multi-tool blade was so dull that he could barely force it into his flesh. How would he ever be able to cut through bone?

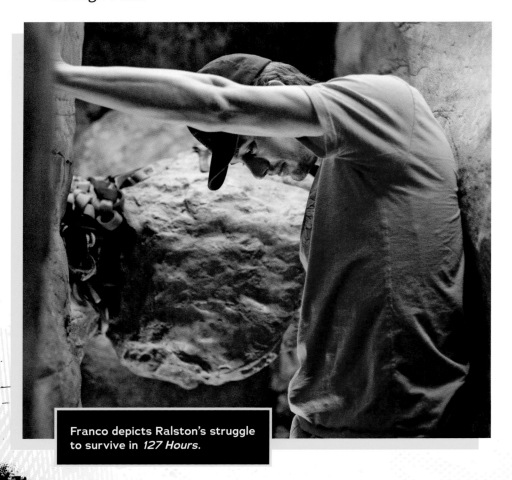

Franco depicts Ralston's struggle to survive in *127 Hours*.

Ralston's name and what he believed was the date he would die are scratched into the canyon wall where he was trapped.

Ralston began to lose hope. He carved his name onto the canyon wall. Next, he recorded the month and year he was born. Finally, he noted the month and year he believed he would die—April 2003.

When dawn broke on Thursday, Ralston was shocked to still be alive. Exhausted and confused, he poked his right hand with his blade. He heard a hissing noise. It almost sounded as if gas was leaking out of his flesh! Without even thinking, he was startled back into his fight to survive.

Suddenly he saw a way to make the amputation work. He had to break his bone *before* he cut. Ralston needed to use the force of his weight to break his arm just above the wrist. Then amputating would be much easier. It was extremely painful, and it took more than an hour. But at 11:32 a.m.—nearly five days after becoming trapped in Bluejohn Canyon—Ralston broke free.

Canyonlands National Park

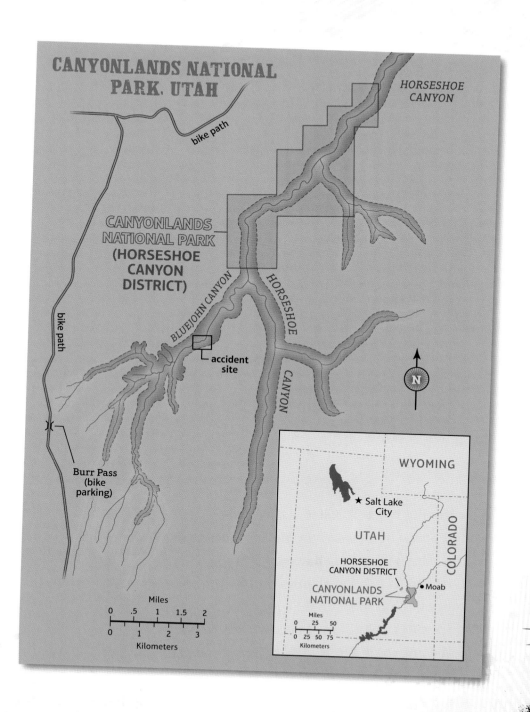

CANYONLANDS NATIONAL PARK, UTAH

HORSESHOE CANYON

bike path

CANYONLANDS NATIONAL PARK (HORSESHOE CANYON DISTRICT)

bike path

BLUEJOHN CANYON

HORSESHOE CANYON

accident site

N

Burr Pass (bike parking)

Miles
0   .5   1   1.5   2
0   1   2   3
Kilometers

WYOMING

★ Salt Lake City

UTAH

COLORADO

HORSESHOE CANYON DISTRICT

CANYONLANDS NATIONAL PARK

● Moab

Miles
0   25   50
0   25   50   75
Kilometers

CHAPTER 4
RESCUE AND RECOVERY

After freeing himself, Ralston felt as though he had been handed a new life. He was in physical shock, but he pushed past his dizziness and exhaustion. He knew he had to get to a hospital as quickly as possible. He grabbed his pack and rappelled 60 feet (18 m) to the canyon floor. Then he walked 5 miles (8 km) until he saw three other hikers. Two of them went to find help. The third stayed with Ralston and gave him food and water.

As Ralston had suspected, his family and friends had reported him missing. They had concluded that he was probably somewhere in the Canyonlands, so a helicopter was already flying nearby, searching for him. Shortly after 3:00 p.m., rescuers picked up Ralston and brought him to a hospital in Moab, Utah. He had lost 40 pounds (18 kg) and a great deal of blood. His recovery was long and difficult, but he was alive.

Ralston spoke at a Colorado hospital in May 2003 about his experience.

REALISTIC RETELLING

The 2010 film *127 Hours* is a retelling of Ralston's experiences in Bluejohn Canyon. The title refers to the time, in hours, that he was trapped. Ralston worked with director Danny Boyle and actor James Franco to make the movie as realistic as possible. Both Boyle and Franco viewed the videos Ralston had recorded so they could better understand his situation. The movie received many positive reviews and several awards.

Ralston (*left*) poses with members of the the cast and crew of *127 Hours* in 2010.

Ralston's story made news headlines around the world. People everywhere were inspired and amazed. Ralston later wrote a book about the experience, and he often gives speeches about survival. Nothing that happened in the canyon lessened Ralston's love of the wilderness. He continues to participate in and lead outdoor expeditions. Ralston is dedicated to preserving natural environments. He also works with an organization that helps people with disabilities enjoy outdoor sports.

Ralston speaks at an event to support the protection of wilderness in Colorado.

FINISHING THE FOURTEENERS

In the summer of 1994, Ralston and a friend hiked Longs Peak in the Colorado Rocky Mountains. It was Ralston's first fourteener, or mountain that is at least 14,000 feet (4.3 km) high. Ralston wanted to explore more fourteeners. In 1997 he promised himself that he would climb each of Colorado's fifty-nine fourteeners—alone and in winter! If Ralston succeeded, he'd be the first mountaineer to do so.

By the time Ralston journeyed into Bluejohn Canyon, he had conquered forty-five of the peaks. After losing an arm, some people would have abandoned the idea of climbing the remaining fourteeners. But Ralston was driven to complete his project.

In 2004 and 2005, Ralston headed back to Colorado's tallest peaks. At times, he felt uncertainty and fear as he climbed the last fourteeners. Hiking with a **prosthetic** arm came with its own unique challenges. But Ralston managed to achieve his goal.

Ralston still hikes alone—but he always leaves his expedition schedule with someone. Despite losing an arm, he remains eager to explore. For him, knowing he has the strength to survive makes it easier to view life's challenges as adventures.

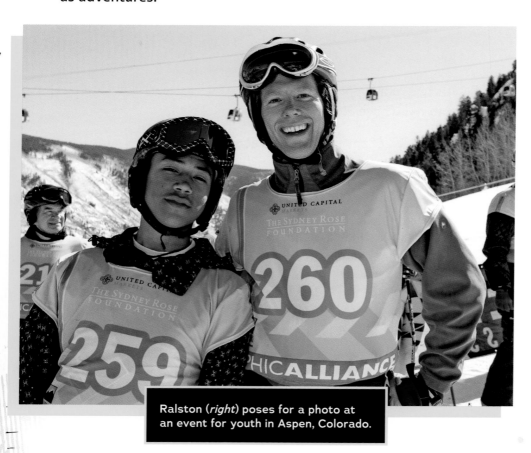

Ralston (*right*) poses for a photo at an event for youth in Aspen, Colorado.

SURVIVING DEADLY SITUATIONS

Every day, people across the globe find themselves facing difficult situations. Each set of circumstances is unique. But there are a few actions that usually help when survival is at stake.

1. Try not to panic. Instead, take a few deep breaths or count backward to calm down.

2. Review your supplies. If you can, record how much food and water you have. Next, create a rationing plan.

3. Make a list of any supplies and equipment you need, and figure out how you can get them. Be creative. For example, try ripping a clean T-shirt into strips for bandages.

4. If you're in a group, think twice before splitting up! If you need to split up to find help, decide how you'll communicate with one another. Plan when and where you'll meet again.

5. If you're alone, attempt to reach someone for help. But don't waste energy or other valuable resources! For example, don't make more phone calls than necessary.

6. If possible, try to keep a record of what's happening. This will help you stay organized and develop a plan.

7. Aron Ralston's story is proof that people are often much stronger than they think. Take one moment at a time, and don't give up!

GLOSSARY

amputate: to cut off a body part, usually as part of a surgery or for a specific medical reason

dehydration: a dangerous physical state that occurs when a person's body doesn't have enough fluid to work properly

expedition: a trip or journey

multi-tool: a small, portable device such as a Swiss Army knife that has several tools attached to one handle

prosthetic: an artificial body part

rappelling: a method of moving down a steep surface by fastening one part of a double rope around a climber's body and another part at a higher point on the surface being climbed

rationing: scheduling the use of a fixed amount of an item, usually to make it last longer

remote: far from towns, cities, or other areas where large numbers of people live and work

tourniquet: a tightly wound cord or bandage to prevent blood loss

FURTHER INFORMATION

Aron Ralston
http://kids.kiddle.co/Aron_Ralston

Aron Ralston Bio
http://www.kidzworld.com/article/28400-aron-ralston-bio

Baxter, Roberta. *Aron Ralston: Pinned in a Canyon*. Mankato, MN: Child's World, 2016.

Canyonlands National Park Facts
http://www.softschools.com/facts/national_parks/canyonlands
_national_park_facts/2903/

Colson, Rob. *Ultimate Survival Guide for Kids*. Buffalo: Firefly Books, 2015.

Oxlade, Chris. *Be a Survivor*. Minneapolis: Hungry Tomato, 2016.

Richardson, Gillian. *Hiking*. New York: AV2 by Weigl, 2014.

What's the Big Sweat about Dehydration?
http://kidshealth.org/en/kids/dehydration.html?WT.ac=
ctg#cater

INDEX

PHOTO ACKNOWLEDGMENTS

Image credits: George Burba/Shutterstock.com, p. 1; Tom Tietz/Shutterstock.com, pp. 4–5; Lisa Maree Williams/Getty Images, p. 5; Anton Pestov/Shutterstock.com, p. 6; Aron Ralston/Wikimedia Commons (CC BY-SA 3.0), p. 7; Whit Richardson/Alamy Stock Photo, p. 8; Eric Strand/Shutterstock.com (rope), p. 9; Keith Homan/Shutterstock.com (bottle), p. 9; Rich/Flickr (CC BY 2.0), p. 9; George Ostertag/Alamy Stock Photo, p. 10; Beth Wald/Aurora Photos/Alamy Stock Photo, pp. 11, 12, 19; David Noton Photography/Alamy Stock Photo, p. 13; Archives du 7e Art/Cloud Eight Films/Alamy Stock Photo, p. 14; modustollens/Shutterstock.com, p. 15; AF Archive/Alamy Stock Photo, pp. 16, 18; Vangelis Vassalakis/Shutterstock.com, p. 17; NPS/Gwen Gerber, p. 20; Laura Westlund/Independent Picture Service, p. 21; Maria Jeffs/Shutterstock.com, p. 22; Gretel Daugherty/Getty Images, p. 23; Jeff Vespa/WireImage/Getty Images, p. 24; Hyoung Chang/The Denver Post/Getty Images, p. 25; robert cicchetti/Shutterstock.com, p. 27; Mary Sue Bonetti/WireImage/Getty Images, p. 28. Design elements: Miloje/Shutterstock.com; Redshinestudio/Shutterstock.com; sl_photo/Shutterstock.com; Khvost/Shutterstock.

Cover: Don Arnold/WireImage/Getty Images (Aron Ralston); George Burba/Shutterstock.com (canyon).